Henry's House

Space

Philip Ardagh

illustrated by Mike Gordon

SCHOLASTIC

For Freddie, of course!
P.A.

Consultant: Fiona Vincent, University of St Andrews

Editorial Director: Lisa Edwards
Senior Editor: Jill Sawyer

Scholastic Children's Books,
Euston House, 24 Eversholt Street,
London NW1 1DB, UK
a division of Scholastic Ltd
London ~ New York ~ Toronto ~ Sydney ~ Auckland
Mexico City ~ New Delhi ~ Hong Kong

First published in the UK by Scholastic Ltd, 2010

Text copyright © Philip Ardagh, 2010
Illustrations copyright © Mike Gordon, 2010
Colour by Carl Gordon

ISBN 978 1407 10721 9

Printed and bound by Tien Wah Press Pte. Ltd, Singapore

10 9 8 7 6 5 4 3 2 1

Papers used by Scholastic Children's Books are made from wood grown in sustainable forests.

**Philip Ardagh and Mike Gordon are regular
visitors to Henry's House. Philip (the one with
the beard) keeps a note of everything that's
going on, and even reads a mind or two. Mike
(the one without the beard) sketches whatever
he sees, however fantastical it may be ... and
together they bring you the adventures of Henry,
an ordinary boy in an extraordinary house!**

Contents

Welcome to Henry's House!

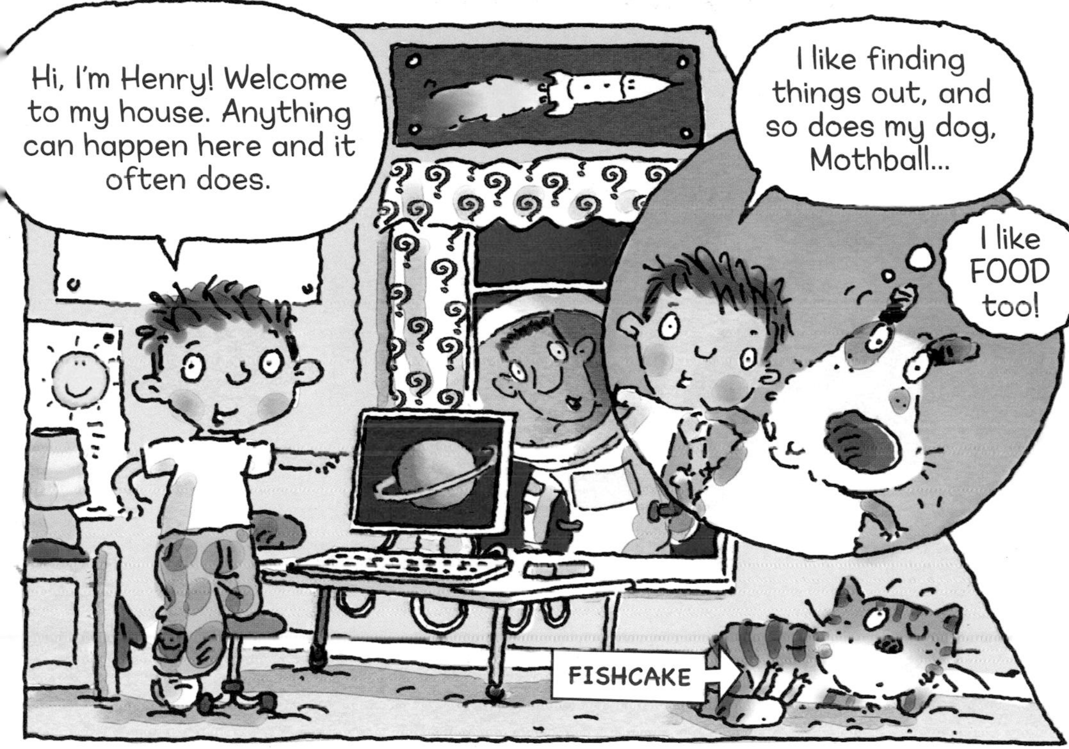

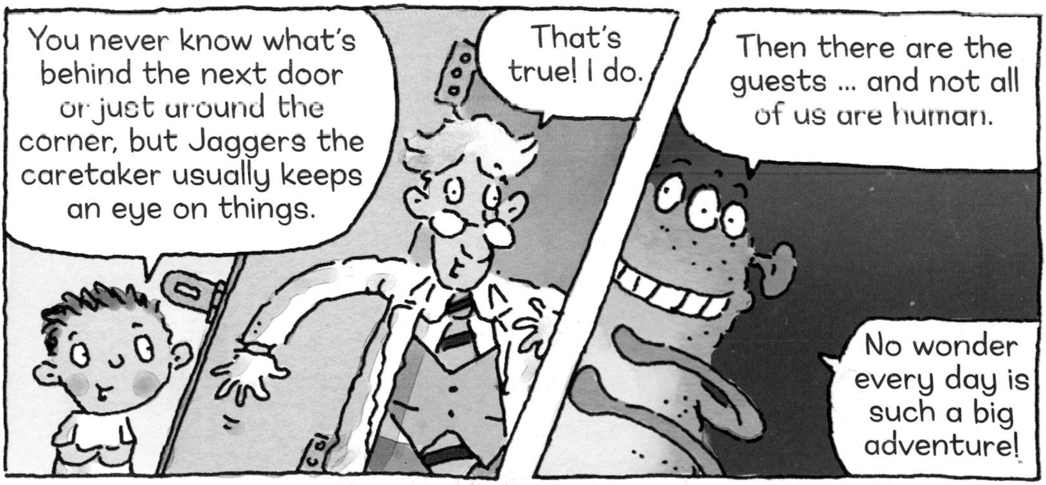

Starry, starry night

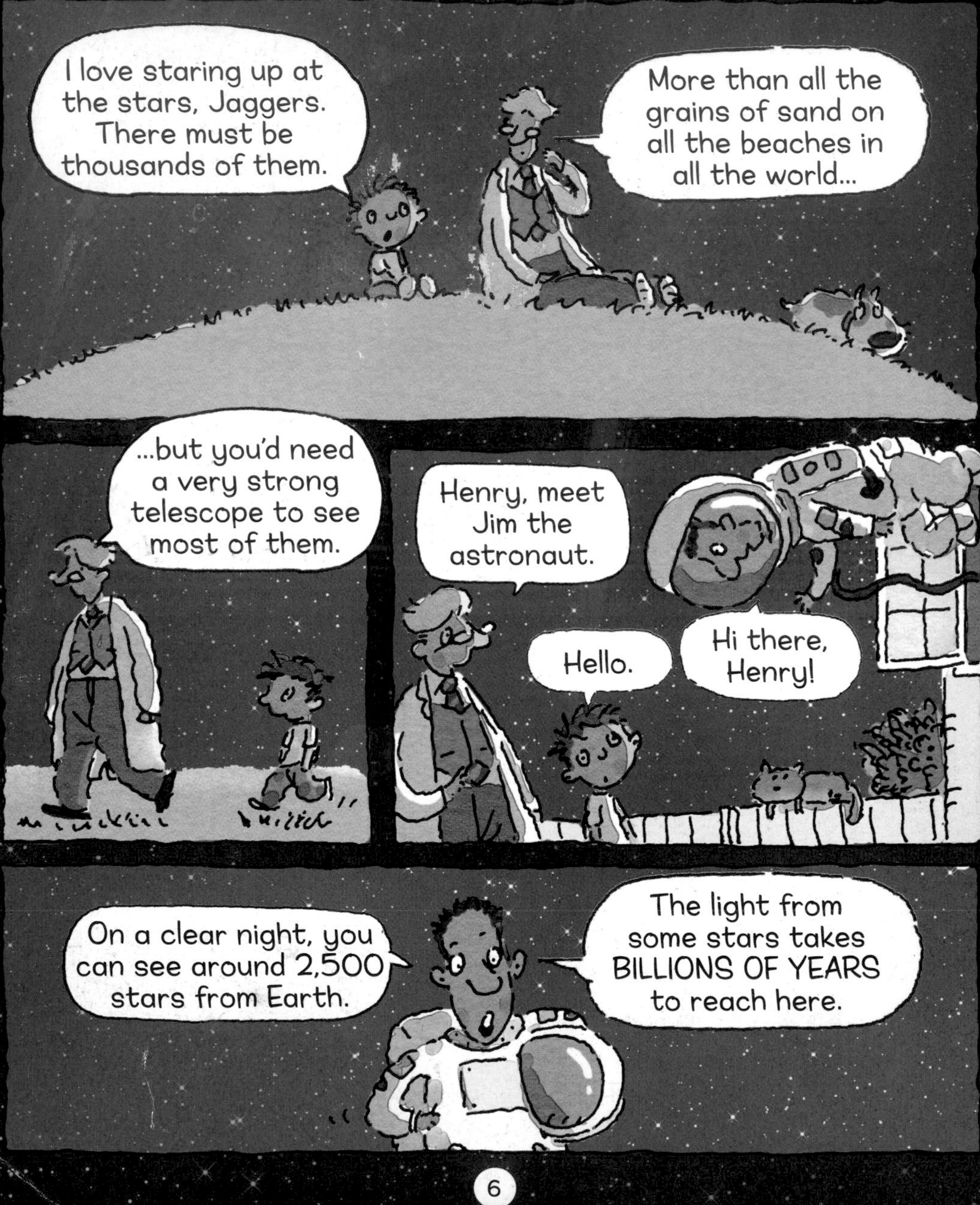

Our Sun is a star. It is a small star compared to some of the stars out there. It seems so big because it's the closest star to Earth.

Stars are huge, glowing balls of burning gases.

Stars don't really "come out at night". They shine just as brightly all the time.

We can't see them in the daytime because of the brightness of the Sun.

Stars only look tiny because they're billions of miles from Earth.

They're also billions of miles apart. In between the stars is what we call SPACE.

Come on. Slip these spacesuits on!

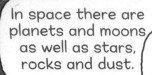

People who study the stars and planets are called astronomers.

Stars are grouped into galaxies.

Our galaxy, the Milky Way, contains BILLIONS of stars.

People first saw patterns in the stars thousands of years ago.

This constellation is called the plough (part of the Great Bear).

This is called Orion.

It's a bit like joining the dots!

Around the Sun

NEPTUNE

PLUTO
(A DWARF
PLANET)

Our solar system is the Sun and the planets that orbit it ... and the moons that orbit those planets too.

Planets orbit the Sun. Moons orbit their planet AND the Sun.

My model doesn't show the distance between the planets. There wasn't room!

Can I orbit your biscuit tin, Cookie?

BEG! BEG!

Pluto

Pluto is 152 times smaller than Earth.

It takes 248 (Earth) years for Pluto to orbit the Sun.

It has at least three moons. (Earth has just one.)

The biggest moon is called Charon.

Pluto is rock in the middle, surrounded by frozen water and then frozen gases.

Experts think that a rock must have hit Pluto, causing a chunk to break away from the dwarf planet. This chunk then began to orbit Pluto, becoming Charon, one of its moons.

Planet Earth

On a tilt

For the half of the Earth that's facing the Sun, it's daytime...

For the half that's facing away from it, it's night.

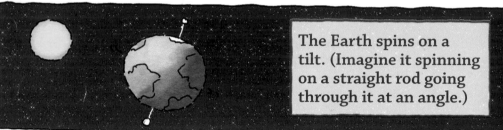

The Earth spins on a tilt. (Imagine it spinning on a straight rod going through it at an angle.)

The coldest time – winter – is when it's tilted furthest away.

The hottest time of year for a country is when it's tilted most directly towards the Sun. That's summer.

Life on Earth

There is a layer of air wrapped around the Earth. This is called the atmosphere.

Without the atmosphere we could not breathe, and more of the Sun's harmful rays would reach Earth.

About two-thirds of the Earth is covered in water.

Earth is the only planet in our solar system with the right atmosphere for plants and animals to exist.

Twinkle, twinkle, little star

Looking at the stars through the Earth's atmosphere is what makes them seem to twinkle.

MOVING AIR IN THE ATMOSPHERE

TWINKLE!

TWINKLE!

EARTH

The Moon

The Moon looks a different shape at different times because the Sun lights up different amounts of it at different times of the month.

The Moon is 50 times smaller than Earth.

It is covered by boulders, dust and craters.

Unlike Earth, the Moon has no atmosphere, no water and no life.

Craters were made when rocks from space crashed into the Moon.

There are deep valleys and high mountains.

THE MOON ON THE MOVE

The Moon spins as it orbits the Earth.

Because of the way it spins, there is one part of the Moon's surface we never see from Earth.

This "unseen" side is called "the dark side of the Moon" (even though it's not really dark)!

The Earth's gravity pulls on the Moon. The Moon's gravity is much weaker, but it pulls on the Earth.

The coming in and going out of the sea – the tides – are caused by the Moon's pull.

The space race

While Leonov was outside the spaceship, his spacesuit swelled up like a big balloon!

This is NOT good!

He couldn't fit back through the door...

Have you been eating out there, Alexel?

UOAHHH!

FSSSSSSST!!!

...so he had to lower the air pressure inside his suit to make it smaller.

That wasn't the end of his troubles. His two-man spacecraft landed back on Earth in snowy mountains 1,200 miles from the proper landing site!

I'm beginning to wish we'd never come!

Blast-off!

BILL BUMBO'S STARGAZING CENTRE

Ah, there you are, Henry! I wondered where you'd got to.

We've been checking out this amazing place!

Have you brought any doggy snacks?

Jim the astronaut was telling me all about who did what FIRST in space!

The Americans were the first and only ones to walk on the Moon, Henry.

Of course landing on the Moon was only part of the challenge.

The real challenge was GETTING BACK TO EARTH ALIVE!!!

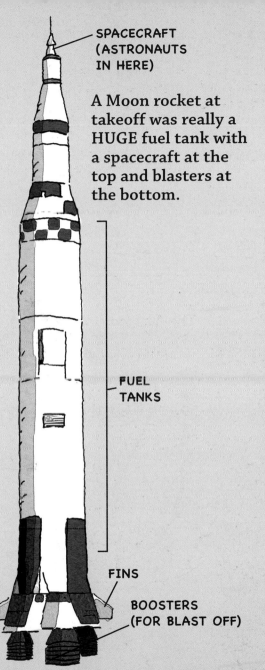

SPACECRAFT
(ASTRONAUTS
IN HERE)

A Moon rocket at takeoff was really a HUGE fuel tank with a spacecraft at the top and blasters at the bottom.

FUEL
TANKS

FINS

BOOSTERS
(FOR BLAST OFF)

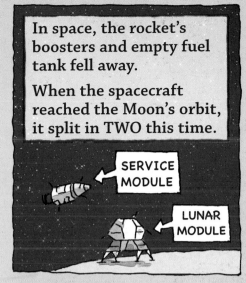

In space, the rocket's boosters and empty fuel tank fell away.

When the spacecraft reached the Moon's orbit, it split in TWO this time.

SERVICE
MODULE

LUNAR
MODULE

To return home:

The lunar module blasted off from Moon and joined up with the service module again.

The astronauts moved into the service module. The lunar module was ejected.

AND ...

... the service module flew home. A tiny capsule came off it and SPLASHED DOWN into the sea.

PARACHUTES

SPLASH!

THE THREE ASTRONAUTS WERE INSIDE

The Russians used to land their space capsules on the ground. In early missions, their astronauts – called cosmonauts – parachuted out first!

BUZZZZ!

What's that noise? It's coming from outside!

29

The shuttle has to "piggy-back" a rocket to get it into space.

Although a space shuttle looks like an aeroplane, it can't take off on a runway.

Space shuttles have never landed on another planet or the Moon.

They have visited space stations and even helped to build one.

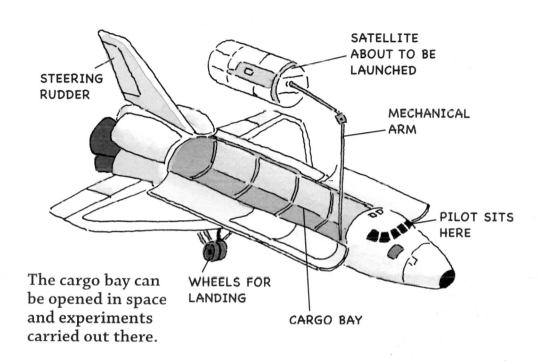

STEERING RUDDER

SATELLITE ABOUT TO BE LAUNCHED

MECHANICAL ARM

PILOT SITS HERE

WHEELS FOR LANDING

CARGO BAY

The cargo bay can be opened in space and experiments carried out there.

That was amazing, Jim!

Sure was, Henry. Now hop in. It's time you and your little doggy friend were in bed.

Little doggy!?!?!

The Sun

The next morning...

Come on, Mothball. It's a beautiful sunny day!

The glow around the Sun is called the corona.

Sometimes ENORMOUS jets of flame shoot out of the Sun. These are called solar flares.

SOLAR FLARE

WARNING: NEVER LOOK STRAIGHT AT THE SUN, EVEN THROUGH DARK GLASSES.

The hottest part of the Sun is its centre, called the core.

The Sun's energy (its heat and light) is produced in the core.

THE CORE

Sunspots are slightly cooler patches.

Ideal for a COOKED breakfast!

SIZZLE!

Although the Sun is 93 million miles from Earth, it only takes about eight minutes for its heat and light to reach us.

You took your time!

Yippee! Breakfast!

Plants need sunshine to help them grow.

The Pistol Star is much bigger and shines MILLIONS of times more brightly than our sun!

YOU ARE MY SUNSHINE!

Eclipse!

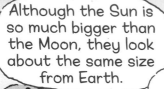

Although the Sun is so much bigger than the Moon, they look about the same size from Earth.

Because the Moon is so much closer?

Exactly, Henry. Let's put these costumes on.

SUN

Sometimes the Moon lines up directly between the Sun and the Earth, so the Sun gets blocked out. This is called a total eclipse of the Sun.

Hank loves his disguises!

MOON

An eclipse of the Sun is called a solar eclipse.

MOON

SUN'S CORONA

Hey! Where did the Sun go?

WARNING: NEVER LOOK STRAIGHT AT THE SUN, EVEN THROUGH DARK GLASSES.

Me again!

EARTH

There are also lunar (Moon) eclipses. These are when the Earth comes between the Sun and the Moon.

The Moon is in the shadow of the Earth so no sunlight can be reflected off it.

SUN

SUNLIGHT

EARTH

MOON

A LUNAR ECLIPSE

Mercury

Which planet is nearest the Sun, Hank?

Don't ask me, Henry! I'm just the handyman!

Why not ask the astronaut or Dr Gubbins?

But we could have a bite to eat first!

Did somebody mention my name?

Mercury is closest to the Sun. This makes it hard to see.

Mercury is the fastest-moving planet in our solar system.

Because it is the closest planet to the Sun, it also has the shortest orbit. It whizzes around the Sun in just 88 Earth days.

VROOM

The planet is named after Mercury, the flying messenger of the Roman gods.

Mercury is very hot and dry in the day and very COLD at night.

No plants or animals can live on it.

It is bare and covered in lots of craters.

The planet is mainly made of iron.

Although Mercury speeds around the Sun, it spins itself very slowly. One day on Mercury lasts 59 Earth days!

CREAK!

You'd need a very big BREAKFAST to keep you going!!

Venus

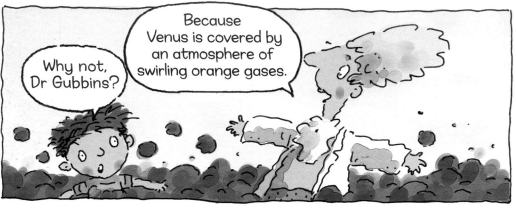

Mars

STOP THAT PLANET!

ROLL!

I'll get it, Dr Gubbins!

It fell down here – WOW! What is this place?

It looks rather like the planet Mars to me, Henry!

Mars may look hot, but it is VERY cold. In winter it is frosty.

There may once have been life here.

Mars is mainly a desert of red sand and broken rocks. Scientists think that there may be frozen water below the surface.

Mars's South Pole is covered in a frozen mixture with ice in it.

Mars was first visited by the Viking 1 space probe in 1976.

SOUTH POLE

AN ICY FROZEN MIXTURE

Humans haven't been to Mars yet. Space probes and robots have.

This robot "roving explorer" is called Opportunity.

It landed on Mars in 2004.

It looks at rocks and takes photos and samples.

Jupiter

A door on the surface of Mars?

Jupiter is the biggest planet in the solar system.

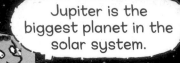

Whoa! That's big!

Jupiter's gravity is very strong because it is such a BIG planet. It has pulled many passing objects into its orbit. Many of these have become Jupiter's moons.

Jupiter has at least 63 moons!

Largest moon
Jupiter's moon Ganymede is bigger than the planet Mercury.

There is a hurricane always raging on Jupiter called the Great Red Spot. It is bigger than the Earth!

GREAT RED SPOT

Jupiter is one of the four "gas giants". They are HUGE planets mostly made up of gas (rather than rocks or liquids).

Jupiter spins around more than TWICE as fast as the Earth does.

Jupiter spins SO fast that it bulges around the middle.

At the centre of Jupiter is its rocky core.

EUROPA   IO

The surface of Jupiter's moon Io is often covered in molten lava. Its moon Europa is covered in ice.

Wheee!

BANG!

BANG!

We seem to have locked ourselves out!

Uh-oh!

Oh no! All the food is on the other side!

UP

VERY, VERY LONG WAY DOWN

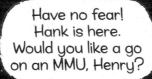

Have no fear! Hank is here. Would you like a go on an MMU, Henry?

WHOA!!!

An MMU (Manned Manoeuvring Unit) lets the astronauts move around in space away from the spacecraft.

The astronaut changes direction using the hand controls.

Gas shoots out of pipes in the back, pushing the astronaut along.

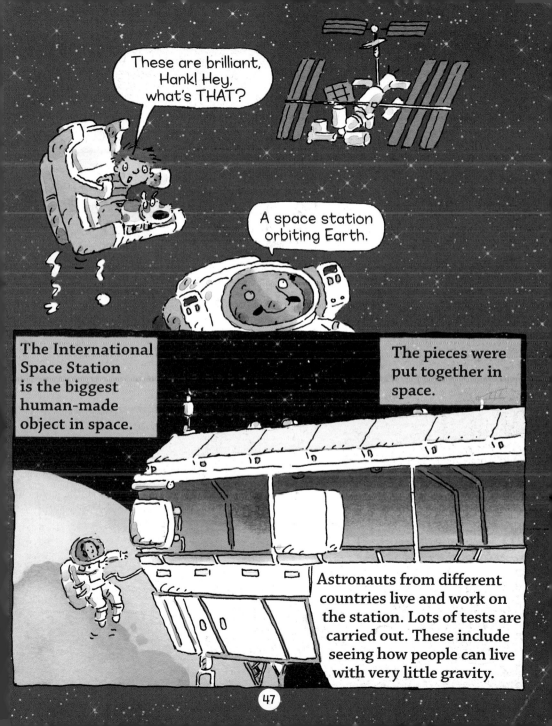

These are brilliant, Hank! Hey, what's THAT?

A space station orbiting Earth.

The International Space Station is the biggest human-made object in space.

The pieces were put together in space.

Astronauts from different countries live and work on the station. Lots of tests are carried out. These include seeing how people can live with very little gravity.

Saturn

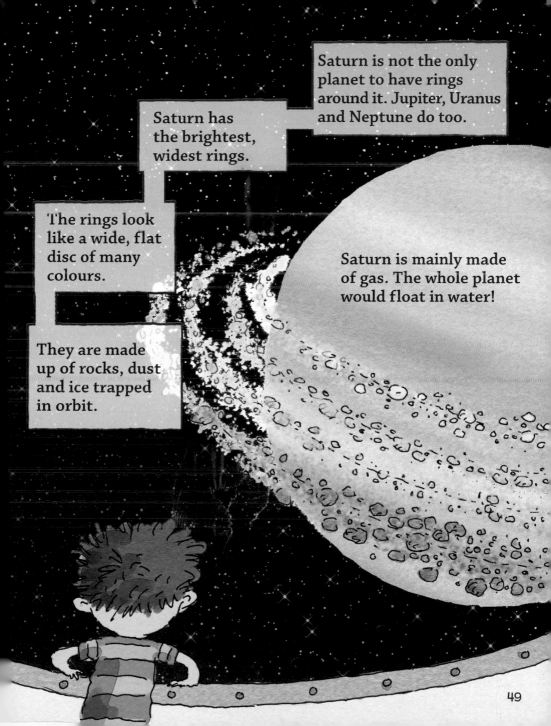

Saturn is not the only planet to have rings around it. Jupiter, Uranus and Neptune do too.

Saturn has the brightest, widest rings.

The rings look like a wide, flat disc of many colours.

Saturn is mainly made of gas. The whole planet would float in water!

They are made up of rocks, dust and ice trapped in orbit.

49

Uranus

THUMP!

ARRGHHH!

OOOPH!

STUMBLE!

WHAT HAPPENED!?!

It feels to me like we've been hit by something very large and thrown sideways ...

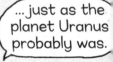

...just as the planet Uranus probably was.

IT'S TRUE!

Night can last for almost 40 years on the parts of Uranus lying away from the Sun.

The planet is made up of many l...

Uranus spins on its side.

...as ...een ... the surface.

Uranus's rings are made of rocks and dust.

GAS AND CRYSTALS

LIQUID

FR...EN LIQUID

SOLID ROCK CORE (ABOUT THE SIZE OF EARTH)

Neptune

Satellites can send TV pictures, radio messages, telephone calls and can even tell you exactly where you are in the world!

Another piece of "space hardware" is the Hubble Space Telescope launched in 1990.

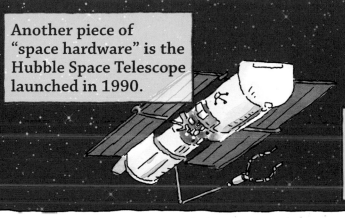

It sends back amazing pictures of planets, stars and even galaxies.

Space probes are sent to explore space. One called Voyager 2 passed the planet Neptune in 1989. It discovered some interesting features.

The Great Dark Spot is a storm. So is the Small Dark Spot.

The Scooter is a cloud that speeds around Neptune every 16 hours.

Neptune is hot inside and cold on its gassy blue surface.

The fastest winds in the solar system are on Neptune. They blow at up to 2,000 kmph! (1,243 mph).

Asteroids, comets and meteoroids

It's lucky that satellite didn't land on anyone!

THOUSANDS of things from space hit the Earth every year, Henry.

Most of them fall into the sea because most of the Earth is covered by water.

Watch the skies!

There are big chunks of rock and metal circling the Sun. They're not big enough to be planets and are called asteroids.

90 per cent of all asteroids circle the Sun in the Asteroid Belt.

Asteroids can be as big as houses, or even mountains!

Sometimes an asteroid crashes into Earth, but this is very unusual.

CRASH!

CRATER

Then there are comets, made up of rock, dust, snow and ice.

Halley's Comet passes Earth every 76 years.

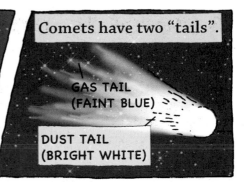

Comets have two "tails".

GAS TAIL
(FAINT BLUE)

DUST TAIL
(BRIGHT WHITE)

Meteoroids are bits of space rock or metal that have broken off asteroids and comets.

If a meteoroid falls through the Earth's atmosphere, it's called a meteor.

If the meteor hits the Earth's surface, it's called a meteorite.

METEOROID

METEOR

METEORITE

So a meteoroid can become a meteor and then a meteorite?

Yes, and around 3,000 meteorites hit the Earth EVERY YEAR.

Some experts think that the dinosaurs were killed out when an asteroid hit the Earth 65 million years ago.

Oh, bother!

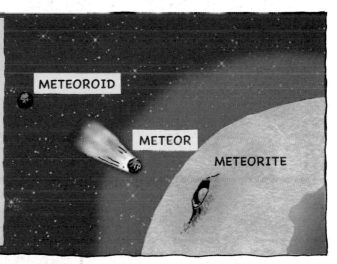

Black holes

So space is lots of space ... with plenty of different things whizzing around in it?

PRECISELY!

SURE IS!

EXACTLY RIGHT!

Take a look in here, Henry! But don't go too close!

What is it?

The most amazing thing, my boy. A black hole made from a collapsed star.

When a star – a sun – runs out of fuel, it stops burning. As it cools, it gets smaller and smaller.

Who turned my light out?

Cool, man!

I'm shrinking!

PLIP

If a really big star gets squeezed so small, its gravity becomes so strong that it even sucks in light ... which is why it looks black.

DR GUBBINS'S BLACK-HOLE "DID-YOU-KNOWS?"

- We can't actually see black holes.
- There aren't any black holes in our solar system.
- No one knows for sure what would happen if we fell in one.

Some scientists think that if a spacecraft went through a black hole it would be spaghettified – stretched long and thin like spaghetti!

Food at long last!

SLURP!

Some scientists think that some black holes might be "worm holes", leading to other universes, Henry.

HENRY!?!?

Ooops!!!

The eight planets in our solar system

MERCURY
Diameter: 4,880 km
Number of moons: 0
Distance from Sun:
58 million km/36 million miles
Length of year: 88 Earth days
Length of day: 59 Earth days
Average surface temp: 167°C

EARTH
Diameter: 12,756 km
Number of moons: 1
Distance from Sun:
150 million km/93 million miles
Length of year: 1 Earth year
Length of day: 1 Earth day
Average surface temp: 15°C

VENUS
Diameter: 12,104 km
Number of moons: 0
Distance from Sun:
108 million km/67 million miles
Length of year: 225 Earth days
Length of day: 243 Earth days
Average surface temp: 464°C

MARS
Diameter: 6,794 km
Number of moons: 2
Distance from Sun:
228 million km/141 million miles
Length of year: 687 Earth days
Length of day: 1.03 Earth days
Average surface temp: –63°C

Look, Mothball. Hank has dressed up as an alien from outer space!

Er, actually, Henry...

It can't be Hank because he's behind you!

WAVE!

THE END

Miles from the Sun:

Because planets don't orbit the Sun in perfect circles, they aren't always the same distance from the Sun. The numbers given here are the AVERAGE distance from the Sun.

JUPITER
Diameter: 143,000 km
Number of moons: at least 63
Distance from Sun:
779 million km/484 million miles
Length of year: 11.9 Earth years
Length of day: 10 Earth HOURS
Average temp: −110°C

URANUS
Diameter: 51,100 km
Number of moons: at least 27
Distance from Sun:
2,872 million km/1,784 million miles
Length of year: 84 earth years
Length of day: 17 Earth HOURS
Average temp: −97°C

SATURN
Diameter: 120,500 km
Number of moons: at least 60
Distance from Sun:
1,434 million km/891 million miles
Length of year: 29 Earth years
Length of day: 11 Earth HOURS
Average temp: −140°C

NEPTUNE
Diameter: 49,500 km
Number of moons: at least 13
Distance from Sun:
4,495 million km/2,793 million miles
Length of year: 165 Earth years
Length of day: 16 Earth HOURS
Average temp: −201°C

Glossary

Air pressure: the push from the air on an object.

Astronaut: someone who travels in space. Russian astronauts are called cosmonauts.

Cargo: goods carried in a ship, aircraft or spacecraft (such as a satellite for launching).

Cargo bay: the part of a ship, aircraft or spacecraft used to store cargo.

Constellation: the patterns and shapes made by stars.

Crater: a large dent or hole in the ground made by a large falling object.

Fuel: a source of energy (such as petrol, rocket fuel or food).

Gravity: the pull felt between two or more objects, such as the Earth and the Moon, holding them together.

WARNING: NEVER LOOK STRAIGHT AT THE SUN, EVEN THROUGH DARK GLASSES.

Hurricane: a powerful storm with very strong winds.

Lunar: to do with a moon (such as a lunar year, or a lunar landing).

Orbit: the path followed by a planet, satellite or star around a bigger object.

Parachute: a large piece of cloth fixed to a person or vehicle – including space capsules – to slow them down, helping to bring them safely down to Earth.

Pilot: the driver of an aircraft or spacecraft.

Rocket: a tube-shaped spacecraft with a pointed end, fired upright into the air at very high speed.

Satellite: an object that moves around a planet, whether it is a moon or a chunk of rock, or human-made, such as a communications satellite (sending and receiving television pictures).

Space probe: a spacecraft without astronauts, designed to explore space and send information back to people on Earth. Some space probes have landed remote-controlled vehicles on other planets.

Spacesuit: the special clothing worn by an astronaut in space, including a helmet and oxygen supply, so that the astronaut can breathe in space, which has no air.

Telescope: a tube-shaped piece of equipment designed to make faraway things – such as stars and planets – look closer and much larger.

Index

Magellan 41
Manned Manoeuvring Unit
(MMU) 46
Mars 10, 42–3, 58
Mercury 10, 38–9, 58
meteorites 54–5
meteoroids 54–5
Milky Way 9
Moon 20–3, 26–7, 29, 31, 36–7,
39
moons 8, 11, 13, 44–5, 58–9

Neptune 11, 49, 52–3, 59
New Moon 20
night 16, 51

observatories 20
Opportunity 43
orbits 8, 11, 13, 22, 44, 47, 49,
52, 59
Orion 9

Pistol Star 35
planets 8–12, 31, 38–45, 49–53
plants 35, 39
Pluto 11–13

rings 48–9, 51

satellites 52
Saturn 10, 48–9, 59
Scooter 53
Small Dark Spot 53

solar flares 32
solar system 10–12, 38, 41, 44,
53, 57–8
space probes 41, 43, 53
space race 24–5
space shuttles 30–1
space stations 31, 47
spacecraft 27, 46, 57
spacesuits 7, 25
stars 6–9, 18, 53, 56
summer 16
Sun 7, 10–11, 15–18, 32–9, 54,
56, 59

telescopes 6, 40, 53
temperature 17, 58–9
Tereshkova, Valentina 24
tides 22

Universe 8, 10, 57
Uranus 11, 49–51, 59

Venus 10, 40–1, 58
Viking 1 43
volcanoes 41
Voyager 2 53

water 18, 21, 42, 54
winds 53
winter 16, 42
worm holes 57

year 15, 58–9

Henry's House

We hope you enjoyed your visit **to Henry's House** **Come back soon!**

Look out for:
- **Knights and Castles**
- **Creepy-crawlies**
- **Egyptians**
- **Dinosaurs**
- **Bodies**

For more facts and fun, visit us at
www.headforhenryshouse.co.uk